CONTENTS

Side Dishes & Snacks

Dessert Recipes

INTRODUCTION

The Mediterranean diet consists of foods that are commonly eaten in the Mediterranean, including an abundance of seafood, fresh fruits, fresh herbs, and fresh vegetables. The Mediterranean diet offers a host of benefits from helping you to lower your blood pressure, lower cholesterol, and even stave off cardiovascular disease, Alzheimer's and Parkinson's disease. Just pair it with moderate exercise, and try to make eating a social event so you're more likely to stick to this diet.

Eating healthy doesn't have to be hard, and you don't have to cook a large amount and just save the rest for later. Many people simply don't' like leftovers because they don't hold the same appeal as fresh food straight from the oven or skillet. With this Mediterranean diet cookbook, you'll find numerous recipes that are perfect for you and your significant other without the need for larger portions.

ABOUT THE DIET

You may be wondering exactly what the Mediterranean diet is, and you need to be aware that it's more of a lifestyle than a normal diet. It's a way of eating that will help you to live a happy, full life. You can lose weight and strengthen your heart while providing yourself with all of the nutrients you need for a long, healthy life. Those that follow this diet often are at a lower risk of cancer, Alzheimer's, enjoy an extended lifespan and overall better cardiovascular health. The Mediterranean diet consists of foods that are rich in healthy oils, filled with vegetable sand fruit, and foods that are low in saturated fat.

This is a heart healthy eating plan that's based on the food that can be found in the Mediterranean, which includes quite a number of countries. It includes pasta, rice, vegetables and fruit, but it does not allow for much red meat. Nuts are also a part of this diet, but they should be limited due to the fact that hey are high in fat and calories.

The Mediterranean diet limits your fat consumption and discourages the eating of saturated or trans-fat. Both types have been linked to heart disease. Grains are often served whole and bread is an important part of the lifestyle, but butter doesn't really play a roll. Wine, however, has a huge place in the Mediterranean diet both in cooking and including a glass with each meal if you are of age. The primary source of fat in this diet are olive oil and fatty fish including herring, mackerel, albacore, tuna, sardines, salmon and trout, which are rich in omega-3 fatty acids.

With the Mediterranean diet, you are giving your body the nutrients and vitamins it needs, so you won't feel hungry. However, it requires a large commitment to eating natural foods, removing temptation, and cooking regular meals. If you love to cook this isn't much of a change, but for those that have few skills in the kitchen it can be a daunting, but well rewarding task. Of course, like with any diet stay well hydrated, and moderate exercise will go a long way!

Foods to Eat

Here is a breakdown of foods that you can eat when using the Mediterranean diet. Of course, it's not a complete list, but this will help you to make a basic shopping plan so that you can get started easily and know what foods you'll be working with.

- **Fruits:** Pears, Grapes, Figs, Peaches, Bananas, Melons, Dates, Oranges, Apples, Strawberries, Raspberries, Blueberries, Blackberries
- **Vegetables:** Spinach, Broccoli, Kale, Onions, Tomatoes, Carrots, Cauliflower, Cucumbers, Brussel Sprouts, Arugula
- **Legumes:** Chickpeas, Beans, Lentils, Peas, Peanuts
- **Nuts & Seeds:** Almonds, Sunflower Seeds, Hazelnuts, Pumpkin Seeds, Cashews, Walnuts
- **Whole Grains:** Whole Oats, Corn, Barley, Brown Rice, Buckwheat, Whole Wheat, Pasta, Rye,
- **Eggs:** Quail, Chicken & Duck
- **Poultry:** Duck, Chicken, Turkey
- **Fish & Seafood:** Sardines, Tuna, Shrimp, Trout, Crab, Clams, Mussels, Oysters, Mackerel, Flounder
- **Tubers:** Sweet Potatoes, Potatoes, Yams, Turnips
- **Dairy:** Greek Yogurt, Cheese, Yogurt
- **Healthy Fats:** Avocados, Olives, Avocado Oil, Olive Oil
- **Herbs & Spices:** Anything Besides Spice Blends

BREAKFAST RECIPES

VEGETABLE OMELET

Serves: 2

Time: 30 Minutes

Ingredients:

- 1/2 Teaspoon Olive Oil
- 1 Cup Fennel Bulbs, Fresh & Sliced Thin
- 1/8 Cup Canned Artichoke Hearts, Rinsed, Drained & Chopped
- 1/8 Cup Green Olives, Pitted & Chopped
- 1 Small Roma Tomato, Chopped
- 3 Eggs
- 1/4 Cup Goat Cheese, Crumbled
- Sea Salt & Black Pepper to Taste

Directions:

1. Start by heating the oven to 325, and then get out an ovenproof skillet. Heat your oil over medium-high heat, and cook your fennel bulb for five minutes.
2. Add in your olives, artichoke hearts, and tomato before cooking for an additional three minutes.
3. Get out a bowl and whisk your eggs, salt and pepper together.
4. Pour this egg mixture over the vegetable mixture, and stir to combine.
5. Cook for two minutes, and then sprinkle evenly with goat cheese.
6. Transfer the skillet to the oven, and bake for five minutes. Your eggs should be completely set.
7. Remove from the skillet, and allow it to cool before slicing.

SALTED BREAKFAST POTATOES

Serves: 2

Time: 15 Minutes

Ingredients:

- 1 Potatoes, Large & Diced
- 1/2 Teaspoon Oregano
- 1/4 Teaspoon Cinnamon
- 1/4 Teaspoon Smoked Paprika
- 1 Rosemary Sprig
- 1 Tablespoon Sunflower Oil
- 1 Tablespoon Butter
- Sea Salt to Taste

Directions:

1. Start by mixing your cinnamon, oregano, paprika and salt together.
2. Wash your potatoes before dicing them, and then rinsing them with cool water. Pat your potatoes dry, and then heat up your butter and oil in a skillet over medium heat. Add in your potatoes, and cook until they're done all the way through, which will take five to ten minutes.
3. Drain, and then season with the salt mixture. Mix well before serving warm.

HUEVOS REVULETOS

Serves: 2

Time: 15 Minutes

Ingredients:

- 2 Eggs
- 1 Tablespoon Butter Spread
- 1/4 Cup Tomatoes, Chopped
- 1/4 Cup Onions, Chopped
- Cilantro, Chopped Fresh to Garnish
- 3 Tablespoons Queso Fresco Cheese, Crumbled

Directions:

1. Melt the butter in a skillet using medium heat, and then once the butter is melted throw in your vegetables. Stir well, and cook for four minutes.
2. Add in the eggs, stirring often to avoid burning. Cook for an additional two minutes or until your eggs are all the way done.
3. Sprinkle with chees and cilantro before serving warm.

BANANA NUT OATMEAL

Serves: 2

Time: 5 Minutes

- 2 Bananas, Peeled
- 1/2 Cup Quick Cooking Oats
- 1 Cup Skim Milk
- 6 Tablespoons Honey, Raw
- 2 Teaspoons Flaxseeds
- 4 Tablespoons Walnuts, Chopped

Directions:

1. Start by combining all ingredients except your bananas in a microwave safe bowl, and cook for two minutes on high.
2. Mash the bananas and stir it into your mixture.
3. Dish between two bowls before serving warm.

EASY MEDITERRANEAN EGGS

Serves: 2

Time: 1 Hour 10 Minutes

Ingredients:

- 3 Yellow Onions
- 4 Eggs, Large
- 1/2 Tablespoon Olive Oil
- 1/2 Tablespoon Butter
- 1 Clove Garlic, Minced
- 3 Tablespoons Tomatoes, Sun Dried
- 3 Ounces Feta Cheese
- Sea Salt & Black Pepper to Taste
- Parsley, Fresh & Chopped
- Ciabatta Rolls, Whole Grain

Directions:

1. Start by heating your oil in a skillet using medium heat, and then add in your onions. Add in your butter, and mix well.
2. Allow them to cook for about an hour. They should be brown and soft, making sure to stir every ten minutes.
3. Add in your tomatoes and garlic, and cook for three minutes more before cracking your eggs on top. Sprinkle with salt and pepper, and then top with feta.
4. Cover with a tight lid, and cook for fifteen minutes without stirring. Serve warm.

MEDITERRANEAN OMELET

Serves: 2

Time: 10 Minutes

Ingredients:

- 1/4 Cup Red Onion, Sliced Thin
- 1/2 Yellow Bell Pepper, Sliced Thin
- 1/2 Red Bell Pepper, Sliced Thin
- 2 Teaspoons Olive Oil, Divided
- 1 Clove Garlic, Minced
- 2 Tablespoons Basil, Fresh & Chopped
- 2 Tablespoons Parsley, Fresh & Chopped + More for Garnish
- 4 Eggs, Beaten
- Sea Salt & Black Pepper

Directions:

1. Get out a heavy skillet and heat up a teaspoon of olive oil using medium heat, and then add in your bell pepper, garlic, and onion. Cook for five minutes, stirring frequently.
2. Add your basil, salt, pepper and parsley. Increase the heat o medium-high, cooking for an additional two minutes.
3. Push the vegetable mix to a plate, and then put the pan back over heat. Heat the remaining oil and pour in your eggs. Tilt until it's coated evenly at the bottom. Cook until the edges are bubbly and the center is nearly dry. This should take roughly five minutes. Flip your omelet.
4. Once your omelet has been flipped, spoon your mixture into one half, and then fold it over.
5. Cut your omelet and serve garnished with parsley.

GARDEN SCRAMBLED EGGS

Serves: 2

Time: 15 Minutes

Ingredients:

- 1/2 Teaspoon Olive Oil
- 1/4 Cup Yellow Squash, Diced
- 14 Cup Green Bell Pepper, Diced
- 1/8 Cup Sweet Onion, Diced
- 3 Cherry Tomatoes, Halved
- 1/2 Tablespoon Basil, Fresh & Chopped
- 1/2 Tablespoon Parsley, Fresh & Chopped
- 4 Eggs, Beaten
- Sea Salt & Black Pepper to Taste

Directions:

1. Get out a nonstick skillet, heating up your olive oil using medium heat.
2. Add in your onion, squash and pepper. Cook until your onion begins to soften which should take about four minutes.
3. Add in your basil, parsley and tomatoes, seasoning with salt and pepper. Cook for a minute more before pouring in your eggs. Cover your pan, and turn the heat down to low.
4. Cook for five to six minutes, making sure that the eggs are set and no longer runny. Cut to serve.

LUNCH RECIPES

GRILLED SARDINES & ARUGULA

Serves: 2

Time: 15 Minutes

Ingredients:

- 1 Bunch Baby Arugula, Trimmed
- 1 Teaspoon Olive Oil
- 8 Ounces Sardines, Fresh, Innards & Gills Removed
- Sea Salt & Black Pepper to Taste
- Lemon Wedges to Garnish

Directions:

1. Start by preparing your grill and then rinsing the arugula. Shake off any excess water, and then place it on a platter. Put the arugula to the side.

2. Rinse the sardines using cold water, and rub them to remove the scales. Wipe them dry, and then get out a bowl. Combine your olive oil and sardine. Toss so that your sardines are well coated.

3. Grill your sardines using high heat for three minutes per side, and then season with salt and pepper. Transfer to plates lined in arugula, and then add your lemon wedges to garnish.

SALMON PANZANELLA

Serves: 2

Time: 10 Minutes

Ingredients:

- 1/2 lb. Center Cut Salmon, Skinned & Sliced into 2 Portions
- 4 Kalamata Olives, Chopped & Pitted
- 1 1/2 Tablespoons Olive Oil
- 1/2 Tablespoon Capers, Chopped
- 1 Tomato, Cut into 1 Inch Pieces
- 1 Slice Stale Bread, Whole Grain, Chopped into 1 Inch Cubes
- 1 1/2 Tablespoons Red Wine Vinegar
- 1 Small Cucumber, Cut into 1 Inch Cubes
- 3 Tablespoons Basil, Fresh & Chopped Fine
- 3 Tablespoons Red Onion, Sliced Thin

Directions:

1. Start by setting your grill to high and then get out a bowl. Whisk your capers, olives, vinegar and pepper until it's well combined, and then add in your onion, cucumber, bread, tomatoes and basil.
2. Oil the grill rack, and then season your salmon with salt and pepper on both sides. Grill the salmon until it's fully cooked, which will take four to five minutes per side.
3. Divide your salad among four plates, topping with salmon.

Serves: 2

Time: 15 Minutes

Ingredients:

- 1/2 Cup Couscous, Whole Wheat
- 4 Ounces Baby Scallops, Tough Muscle Removed
- 4 Ounces Shrimp, Peeled & Deveined
- 2 Teaspoons Olive Oil
- 1 Clove Garlic, Minced
- 1 Onion, Chopped
- 1/2 Teaspoon Fennel Seeds
- 1/2 Teaspoon Thyme
- 1/4 Cup Vegetable Broth
- Sea Salt & Black Pepper to Taste
- 1 Cup Tomatoes, Canned, Diced & No Salt Added with Juice
- Pinch Saffron Threads, Crumbled

Directions:

1. Start by getting out a saucepan, and heat your oil over medium heat. Add in your onion, and cook for three minutes. Make sure to stir regularly to keep it from burning. Add in your garlic, pepper, thyme, salt, saffron and fennel seeds. Cook for about a half a minute more.

2. Stir in the tomatoes and broth, and then bring it all to a simmer. Cover, reducing the heat and simmering for two minutes more.

3. Increase the heat to medium, and then stir in the scallops, cooking for an additional two minutes. Stir occasionally to keep it from sticking.

4. Add the shrimp, cooking for two minutes more.

5. Stir in your couscous, and then cover and remove your pan from heat. Allow it to stand for five minutes before fluffing to serve warm.

GREEK SALMON BURGERS

Serves: 2

Time: 20 Minutes

- 2 Ciabatta Rolls, Toasted
- 1/8 Cup Feta Cheese, Crumbled
- Sea Salt & Black Pepper to Taste
- 1/4 Cup Cucumber Slices
- 1/4 Cup Panko
- 1 Small Egg Whites
- 1/2 lb. Salmon Fillets, Skinless & Chopped into 2 Inch Pieces

Directions:

1. Get out a food processor pulsing the egg white, panko and salmon together until the salmon is chopped fine.
2. Form into two patties, and then season with salt and pepper.
3. Heat the grill to medium-high, and then grease the grill. Cook the patties for five to seven minutes per side and toast the ciabatta rolls.
4. Top with cucumber slices before serving warm.

TUNA PASTA WITH ARTICHOKES

Serves: 2   Time: 25 Minutes

Ingredients:

- 4 Ounces Tuna Steak, Sliced into 2 Pieces
- 1 Teaspoon Lemon Zest, Fresh
- 2 Tablespoons Olive Oil
- Sea Salt & Black Pepper to Taste
- 1 Teaspoon Rosemary, Fresh & Chopped
- 1/8 Cup Green Olives, Chopped

- 5 Ounces Artichoke Hearts, Frozen & Thawed
- 3 Ounces Penne Pasta, Whole Wheat
- 1 Cup Grape Tomatoes
- 2 Cloves Garlic, Minced
- 1 Tablespoon Lemon Juice, Fresh
- 1/4 Cup White Wine
- 1/8 Cup Basil, Fresh & Chopped

Directions:

1. Start by heating your grill to medium-high heat, and then get out a large pot of water. Bring your water to a boil.

2. Get out a bowl and toss the tuna pieces in with lemon zest, half your rosemary, half your oil, a dash of salt and pepper. And then grill for three minutes per side before putting it on a plate. Cut it to bite sized pieces when the tuna is cool enough to handle.

3. Cook your pasta in the boiling water according to package instructions and then drain when finished.

4. Heat the remaining oil in a skillet using medium heat, adding in your artichoke hearts, remaining rosemary, olives and garlic. Cook for four minutes more, and stir often to keep from burning. Add your wine and tomatoes, and then bring it to a boil for three minutes more. Your wine should have reduced some and your tomatoes should be broken down. Stir in your pasta, lemon juice and tuna pieces. Add another dash of salt, and cook for two minutes. Garnish with a ¼ cup of basil.

CHICKEN & GARBANZO SALAD

Serves: 2

Time: 15 Minutes

Ingredients:

- 4.5 Ounces Chicken Breast, Cooked & Chopped
- 7 Ounces chickpeas
- 1/2 Cup Cucumber, Seeded & Chopped
- 1/8 Cup Mint, Fresh & Chopped
- 1/8 Cup Green Onions, Chopped
- 1/4 Cup Plain Yogurt, Fat Free
- 2 Cloves Garlic, Minced
- 1 Cups Baby Spinach
- 1/6 Cup Feta Cheese, Crumbled
- Sea Salt & Black Pepper to Taste
- 2 Lemon Wedges

Directions:

1. Start by combining all of your ingredients except for your feta, spinach and lemon wedges. Fold in the feat and spinach leaves next.
2. Add in your lemon wedges, and then serve.

MEDITERRANEAN TUNA SALAD

Serves: 2

Time: 15 Minutes

Ingredients:

- 1/4 Cup Lemon Juice, Fresh
- 1/4 Cup Parsley, Fresh & Chopped
- 2 Teaspoons Capers
- 1/2 Red Bell Pepper, Diced Fine
- 1/4 Cup Red Onion, Chopped
- 1 Can Light Tuna, Water Packed & 6 Ounces Each
- 10 Ounces Chickpeas, Canned
- 3/4 Teaspoon Rosemary, Fresh & Chopped Fine
- 2 Tablespoons Olive Oil
- 4 Cups Mixed Salad Greens
- Sea Salt & Black Pepper to Taste

Directions:

1. Combine your tuna, onion, capers, pepper, beans, parsley, rosemary, a tablespoon of oil and your 1/8 cup lemon juice. Season with a dash of salt and pepper, and mix well.
2. Mix your remaining lemon juice, salt and oil in a bowl, adding your salad greens, and toss to coat before serving.

FLANK STEAK & SPINACH SALAD

Serves: 2

Time: 30 Minutes

Ingredients:

- 1/2 lb. Flank Steak
- 1/2 Teaspoon Olive Oil
- 1 Tablespoon Garlic Powder
- Sea Salt & Black Pepper to Taste
- 2 Cups Baby Spinach
- 5 Cremini Mushrooms, Sliced
- 5 Cherry Tomatoes, Halved
- 1/4 Red Bell Pepper, Sliced Thin
- 1 Small Red Onion, Sliced Thin

Directions:

1. Get out a baking sheet and line it with foil, and then preheat your broiler.
2. Rub the steak down with olive oil, salt, pepper and garlic, allowing it to marinate for ten minutes before putting it on the pan under your broiler. Broil for five minutes, and allow it to rest for ten.
3. Get out a large bowl and combine your tomatoes, onion, mushrooms, spinach and bell pepper. Toss to combine.
4. Serve with steak sliced on top.

Serves: 2

Time: 15 Minutes

Ingredients:

- 1/4 Cup Balsamic Vinegar
- 1 Teaspoon Lemon Juice, Fresh
- 1/4 Cup Olive Oil
- 2 Grilled Chicken Breasts, Boneless, Skinless & Sliced
- 1/2 Cup Red Onion, Sliced Thin
- 8 Kalamata Olives, Halved & Pitted
- 10 Cherry Tomatoes, Halved
- 2 Cups Romaine Lettuce, Chopped Roughly
- 1/2 Cup Feta Cheese
- Sea Salt & Black Pepper to Taste

Directions:

1. Get out a bowl and combine your lemon juice and vinegar, stirring until it is well combined. Whisk your olive oil in slowly, and continue to whisk until well blended. Add your salt and pepper and whisk again.
2. Add in your onion, tomatoes, olives and chicken. Stir well, and then cover. Allow it to chill for at least two hours or even overnight.
3. Divide the lettuce between two plates, and top with half of your vegetables and chicken. Sprinkle your feta cheese over both plates before serving.

CHEESE STUFFED TOMATOES

Serves: 2

Time: 30 Minutes

Ingredients:

- 1/2 Cup Yellow Onion, Diced
- 1/2 lb. White Mushrooms, Sliced
- 2 Cloves Garlic, Minced
- 4 Large Tomatoes, Ripe
- 1 Tablespoon Olive Oil
- 1 Tablespoon Basil, Fresh & Chopped
- 1 Tablespoon Oregano, Fresh & Chopped
- 1 Cup Mozzarella Cheese, Shredded & Part Skim
- 1 Tablespoon Parmesan Cheese, Grated
- Sea Salt & Black Pepper to Taste

Directions:

1. Start by heating the oven to 375 before getting out a baking pan. Line it in foil, and then rinse your tomatoes. Slice a sliver from the bottom of each so they can stand on the tray, and then cut a slice from the top of each about a half an inch. Scoop the pulp out, placing it in a bowl.
2. Get a skillet out and heat up your olive using medium heat. Sauté your mushrooms, garlic, onion, basil and oregano for five minutes. Season with salt and pepper. Transfer this to a bowl, and blend with your tomato pulp. Stir in your cheese.
3. Fill each tomato loosely with the mix, topping with parmesan. Bake for fifteen to twenty minutes. Your cheese should be bubbly.

TOMATO & PASTA BOWL

Serves: 2

Time: 20 Minutes

Ingredients:

- 4 Ounces Linguine, Whole Grain
- 1 clove Garlic, Minced
- 1/2 Tablespoon Olive Oil
- 1/8 Cup Yellow Onion, Chopped
- 1/2 Teaspoon Oregano, Fresh & Chopped
- 1/2 Teaspoon Tomato Paste
- 4 Ounces Cherry Tomatoes, Halved
- 1/2 Tablespoon Parsley, Fresh & Chopped
- 1/4 Cup Parmesan Cheese, Grated
- Sea Salt & Black Pepper to Taste

Directions:

1. Get out a saucepan to boil water over high heat, cooking the linguine according the package. Drain, and reserve a half a cup of the pasta water, but do not rinse your pasta.
2. Get out a heavy skillet and place it over medium-high heat to heat up your olive oi. Sauté your oregano, garlic and onion for five minutes.
3. Add in the tomato paste, ¼ cup of pasta water, and season with salt and pepper. Cook for a minute.
4. Stir in your tomatoes next as well as your cooked pasta, adding more pasta water if needed.
5. Top with parmesan and parsley before serving.

GARLIC BROILED SARDINES

Serves: 2

Time: 15 Minutes

Ingredients:

- 2 Cloves Garlic, Minced
- 1 Tablespoon Olive Oil (Only if your Sardines are packed in water)
- 1/4 Teaspoon Red Pepper Flakes
- Sea Salt & Black Pepper to Taste
- 2 Cans Sardines (3.25 Ounces Each)

Directions:

1. Start by preheating your broiler before getting out a baking dish. Line the baking dish with foil before arranging your sardines on the bottom in a single layer.
2. Combine your olive oil, red pepper flakes and garlic in a bowl, spooning it over the sardines.
3. Sprinkle sea salt and black pepper over them, and then broiler for three minutes. Serve warm.

FRUITY CHICKEN SALAD

Serves: 2

Time: 15 Minutes

Ingredients:

- 1/4 Cup Celery, Diced
- 1/4 Cup Red Onion, Diced
- 1/2 Cup Cranberries, Dried
- 2 Cups Chicken Breast, Cooked & Chopped
- 2 Granny Smith Apples, Peeled, Cored & Diced
- 2 Tablespoons Honey Dijon Mustard
- 1 Tablespoons Olive Oil Based Mayonnaise
- Sea Salt & Black Pepper to Taste

Directions:

1. Get outa bowl and combine your cranberries, chicken, apples, celery and onion. Mix until well combined.
2. Get out another bowl and mix your mayonnaise, salt, pepper and mustard. Whisk well until it's blended. Stir your dressing into the chicken mixture, making sure it's well combined before serving.

DINNER RECIPES

MUSTARD TROUT WITH APPLES

Serves: 2

Time: 1 Hour 5 Minutes

Ingredients;

- 1 Tablespoon Olive Oil
- 1 Small Shallot, Minced
- 2 Lady Apples, Halved
- 4 Trout Fillets, 3 Ounces Each
- 1 1/2 Tablespoons Bread Crumbs, Plain & Fine
- 1/2 Teaspoon Thyme, Fresh & Chopped
- 1/2 Tablespoon Butter, Melted & Unsalted
- 1/2 Cup Apple Cider
- 1 Teaspoon Light Brown Sugar
- 1/2 Tablespoon Dijon Mustard
- 1/2 Tablespoon Capers, Rinsed
- Sea Salt & Black Pepper to Taste

Directions:

1. Start by heating your oven to 375, and then get out a small bowl. Combine your bread crumbs, shallot and thyme before seasoning with salt and pepper.
2. Add in the butter, and mix well.

3. Put the apples cut side up in a baking dish, and then sprinkle with sugar. Top with bread crumbs, and then pour half of your cider around the apples, covering the dish. Bake for a half an hour.

4. Uncover, and then bake for twenty more minutes. The apples should be tender but your crumbs should be crisp. Remove the apples from the oven.

5. Turn the broiler on, and then put the rack four inches away. Pat your trout down, and then season with salt and pepper. Brush your oil on a baking sheet, and then put your trout with the skin side up. Brush your remaining oil over the skin, and broil for six minutes. It should be cooked all the way through. Repeat the apples on the shelf right below the trout. This will keep the crumbs from burning, and it should only take two minutes to heat up.

6. Get out a saucepan, and whisk your remaining cider, capers, and mustard together. Add more cider if necessary to thin, and cook for five minutes on medium-high. It should have a sauce like consistency. Spoon the juices over the fish, and serve with an apple on each plate.

CHICKEN MILANO

Serves: 2

Time: 30 Minutes

Ingredients:

- 4.5 Ounces Green Beans, Frozen
- 1/2 Teaspoon Red Pepper Flakes, Crushed
- 14 Ounces Stewed Tomatoes, Canned & Drained
- 1/2 Teaspoon Italian Style Seasoning
- 1/2 Tablespoon Vegetable Oil
- 1 Clove Garlic, Crushed
- 2 Chicken Breast Halves, Skinless & Boneless
- Sea Salt & Black Pepper to Taste

Directions:

1. Use a large skillet over medium-high heat to heat up your vegetable oil. Once your oil is hot add your chicken, and season with red pepper flakes, salt, pepper, garlic and Italian seasoning.
2. Cook for five minutes before adding the tomatoes in. cook for an additional five minutes, and then add in your green beans. Stir well.
3. Cover, and then reduce the heat to medium-low. Allow it to simmer for twenty minutes before serving warm.

SICILIAN LEMON CHICKEN

Serves: 2

Time: 1 Hour 10 Minutes

Ingredients:

- 2 Tablespoons Olive Oil
- 2 Chicken Breast Halves, Boneless & Skinless
- 8 Ounces Angel Hair Pasta
- 1/3 Cup Golden Raisins
- 2 Sprigs Fresh Basil
- 1/2 Lemon, Juice & Zested
- 1/2 Onion, Sliced Thin
- 2 Tablespoons Parmesan Cheese
- 1/4 Teaspoon Cayenne Pepper
- 1/2 Tablespoons Garlic, Minced
- 1 Tablespoon Black Olives, Chopped
- 1 Tablespoon Pine Nuts
- 1 Bay Leaf
- 8 Ounces Tomatoes, Diced, Canned & Drained
- 1/4 Teaspoon Oregano
- 1/2 Tablespoon Balsamic Vinegar
- 1 Tablespoon Fresh Basil, Chopped
- 1/2 Teaspoon Sugar
- Sea Salt & Black Pepper to Taste

Directions:

1. Soak the raisins in warm water for ten minutes. They should be plump, and then drain them. Set the raisins to the side.

2. Heat your olive oil over medium-high heat in a saucepan, and then once it's hot add in your lives, pine nuts, garlic and onion. Season with bay leaf, cayenne and oregano. Cook for five minutes. Your onion should be softened.

3. Stir in your tomatoes, seasoning with salt and pepper. Cook for another five minutes.

4. Add in your raisins, sugar, and balsamic vinegar. Cook for five minutes more. The sauce should be thickened. Remove your basil and bay leaf, and then cover to keep warm.

5. Bring a pot of water to a boil, and then cook your pasta for about ten minutes. They should be al dente, and then drain the pasta.

6. Heat another half tablespoon of olive oil using medium heat in a different skillet, cooking your chicken with lemon juice. Make sure it's browned on both sides, which will take roughly fifteen minutes. Allow it to rest on a plate for five more minutes.

7. Slice the chicken breast again the grain, and try to make thin slices. Divide your pasta, and then top with your chicken slices and tomato sauce. Sprinkle on your parmesan, lemon zest and garnish with basil before serving warm.

Serves: 2

Time: 1 Hour 5 Minutes

Ingredients:

- 2 Small Carrots, Diced
- 1 Clove Garlic, Minced
- 1/2 Tablespoon Olive Oil
- 2 Chicken Legs, Skinned & Cut into Drumstick and Thighs
- 1/2 Cup Chicken Broth, Low Sodium
- 1 Tablespoon Ginger, Fresh & Chopped
- 1/2 Cup Dry White Wine
- 1/2 Cup Water
- 1/4 Cup Green Olives, Pitted & Chopped
- 3 Tablespoons Raisins
- 1/3 Cup Chickpeas, Canned, Drained & Rinsed
- 2 Sprigs Thyme, Fresh

Directions:

1. Start by heating your oven to 350, and then get out a Dutch oven or oven safe skillet. Heat your olive oil using medium heat, and then place the chicken in the skillet. Make sure that the pan isn't overcrowded. Sauté for five minutes per side, which should make your chicken crisp. Transfer it to a plate, and place the chicken to the side for now.

2. Reduce the heat to medium-low, throwing in your garlic, ginger, onion and carrots. Sauté, and make sure to stir frequently as to not burn your onion. Your onion should soften in five minutes, and then throw in your wine, broth and water. Bring it to a boil to deglaze the pan.

3. Add your chicken back in, and then add in your thyme. Bring it up to a boil again, and then place it in the oven. Cook for forty-five minutes.

4. Take it out of the oven, and stir in your olives, raisins, and chickpeas. Return it to the oven, braising while uncovered for twenty minutes. Discard the thyme before serving.

LAMB & COUSCOUS SALAD

Serves: 2

Time: 25 Minutes

Ingredients:

- 1/2 Cup Water
- 1/2 Tablespoon Garlic, Minced
- 1 1/4 lb. Lamb Loin Chops, Trimmed
- 1/4 Cup Couscous, Whole Wheat
- Pinch Sea Salt
- 1/2 Tablespoon Parsley, Fresh & Chopped Fine
- 1 Tomato, Chopped
- 1 Teaspoon Olive Oil
- 1 Small Cucumber, Peeled & Chopped
- 1 1/2 Tablespoons Lemon Juice, Fresh
- 1/4 Cup Feta, Crumbled
- 1 Tablespoon Dill, Fresh & Chopped Fine

Directions:

1. Get out a saucepan and bring the water to a boil.
2. Get out a bowl and mix your garlic, salt and parsley. Press this mixture into the side of each lamb chop, and then heat your oil using medium-high heat in a skillet.

3. Add the lamb, cooking for six minutes per side. Place it to the side, and cover to help keep the lamb chops warm.

4. Stir the couscous into the water once it's started to boil, returning it to a boil before reducing it to low so that it simmers. Cover, and then cook for about two minutes more. Remove from heat, and allow it to stand uncovered for five minutes. Fluff using a fork, and then add in your tomatoes, lemon juice, feta and dill. Stir well. Serve on the side of your lamb chops.

SPICED TURKEY & GRAPEFRUIT RELISH

Serves: 2

Time: 15 Minutes

Ingredients:

Relish:

- 1 Grapefruit, Seedless
- 1 Small Shallot, Minced
- 1 Teaspoon Red Wine Vinegar
- 1 Teaspoon Honey, Raw
- 1/2 Small Avocado, Pitted, Peeled & Diced
- 1 Tablespoon Cilantro, Fresh & Chopped

Spiced Turkey:

- 2 Turkey Cutlets, 8 Ounces Each
- 1/2 Teaspoon Five Spice Powder
- 1 Tablespoon Chili Powder
- 1 Tablespoon Olive Oil
- Pinch Sea Salt, Fine

Directions:

1. Start by peeling your grapefruit and cutting away the white pith. Cut the fruit into segments, making sure to remove the membrane. Squeeze any juice that remains in a bowl, and then add in your vinegar, shallots, honey, avocado and cilantro. Toss to combine, and then set it to the side.
2. Combine the chili powder, salt and five spice powder, coating your turkey in the mixture.

3. Heat the oil in a skillet over medium-high heat, cooking your turkey for three minutes per side. It should still be pink in the middle when you remove it from the pan.

4. Divide your turkey between plates, adding your relish on the side to serve.

GREEK CHICKEN PENNE

Serves: 2

Time: 20 Minutes

Ingredients:

- 1 Clove Garlic, Minced
- 8 Ounces Penne Pasta
- 1/2 lb. Chicken Breast Halves, Boneless, Skinless & Chopped
- 1/4 Cup Red Onion, Chopped
- 3/4 Tablespoon Butter
- 8 Ounces Artichoke Hearts, Canned
- 1 Small Tomato, Chopped
- 1 1/2 Tablespoons Parsley, Fresh & Chopped
- 1/4 Cup Feta Cheese, Crumbled
- 1 Tablespoon Lemon Juice, Fresh
- 1/2 Teaspoon Oregano
- Sea Salt & Black Pepper to Taste

Directions:

1. Start by cooking your pasta per package instructions so that it's al dente. Drain your pasta and place it to the side.

2. Get out a skillet and melt your butter over medium-high heat. Cook your onion and garlic for two minutes before adding in your chicken. Cook for six more minutes, making sure to stir occasionally to keep it from burning.

3. Reduce the heat to medium-low before draining and chopping your artichoke hearts. Throw them in the skillet with your parsley, tomato, oregano, lemon juice, feta cheese and drained pasta. Heat all the ay through and cook for three minutes.

4. Season with salt and pepper, and serve warm.

Serves: 2

Time: 20 Minutes

Ingredients:

- 1/4 Teaspoon Black Pepper
- 1/2 Cup Dry Bread Crumbs
- 1 Egg
- 3/4 lb. Chicken Breast Halves, Skinless & Boneless (Pounded 3/4 Inch Thick & Sliced)
- 3 Tablespoons Capers
- 1 Lemon, Cut into Wedges

Directions:

1. Start by beating your eggs with your pepper, mixing in the bread crumbs.
2. Get out a skillet and heat your olive oil using medium heat. Dip the chicken into the egg mixture, spreading the bread crumbs into the chicken, shaking any lose ones off. Fry the chicken in the pan for about eight minutes per side so that it becomes golden brown.
3. Drizzle your chicken with caper juice, and serve with lemon wedges.

GNOCCHI WITH SHRIMP

Serves: 4

Time: 20 Minutes

Ingredients:

- 1/2 lb. Shrimp, Peeled & Deveined
- 1/4 Cup Shallots, Sliced
- 1/2 Tablespoon + 1 Teaspoon Olive Oil
- 8 Ounces Shelf Stable Gnocchi
- 1/2 Bunch Asparagus, Cut into Thirds
- 3 Tablespoons Parmesan Cheese
- 1 Tablespoon Lemon Juice, Fresh
- 1/3 Cup Chicken Broth
- Sea Salt & Black Pepper to Taste

Directions:

1. Start by heating a half a tablespoon of oil over medium heat, and then add in your gnocchi. Cook while stirring often until they turn plump and golden. This will take from seven to ten minutes. Place them in a bowl.

2. Heat your remaining teaspoon of oil with your shallots, cooking until they begin to brown. Make sure to stir, but this will take two minutes. Stir in the broth before adding your asparagus. Cover, and cook for three to four minutes.

3. Add the shrimp, seasoning with salt and pepper. Cook until they are pink and cooked through, which will take roughly four minutes.

4. Return the gnocchi to the skillet with lemon juice, cooking for another two minutes. Stir well, and then remove it from heat.

5. Sprinkle with parmesan, and let it stand for two minutes. Your cheese should melt. Serve warm.

SHRIMP SAGANAKI

Serves: 2

Time: 45 Minutes

Ingredients:

- 1/2 lb. Shrimp with Shells
- 1 Small Onion, Chopped
- 1/2 Cup White Wine
- 1 Tablespoon Parsley, Fresh & Chopped
- 8 Ounces Tomatoes, Canned & Diced
- 3 Tablespoons Olive Oil
- 4 Ounces Feta Cheese
- Cubed Salt
- Dash Black Pepper
- 14 Teaspoon Garlic Powder

Directions:

1. Get out a saucepan and then pour in about two inches of water, bringing it to a boil. Boil for five minutes, and then drain but reserve the liquid. Set both the shrimp and the liquid to the side.
2. Heat two tablespoons of oil up next, and when heated add in your onions. Cook until the onions are translucent. Mix in your parsley, garlic, wine, olive oil and tomatoes. Simmer for a half hour, and stir until it's thickened.
3. Remove the legs of the shrimp, pulling off the shells, head and tail.
4. Add the shrimp and shrimp stock into the sauce once it's thickened. Bring it to a simmer for five minutes, and then add the feta cheese.
5. Let it stand until the cheese starts to melt, and then serve warm.

MEDITERRANEAN SALMON

Serves: 2

Time: 30 Minutes

Ingredients:

- 2 Salmon Fillets, Skinless & 6 Ounces Each1
- 1 Cup Cherry Tomatoes
- 1 Tablespoon Capers
- 1/4 Cup Zucchini, Chopped Fine
- 1/8 Teaspoon Black Pepper
- 1/8 Teaspoon Sea Salt, Fine
- 1/2 Tablespoon Olive Oil
- 1.25 Ounces Ripe Olives, Sliced

Directions:

1. Start by heating your oven to 425, and then sprinkle your salt and pepper over your fish on both sides. Place the fish in a single layer on your baking dish after coating your baking dish using cooking spray.
2. Combine the tomatoes and remaining ingredients, spooning the mixture over your fillets, and then bake for twenty-two minutes. Serve warm.

Serves: 2

Time: 45 Minutes

Ingredients:

- 2 Cloves Garlic, Chopped
- 4 Ounces Linguine, Whole Wheat
- 1 Tablespoon Olive Oil
- 14 Ounces Tomatoes, Canned & Diced
- 1/2 Tablespoon Shallot, Chopped
- 1/4 Cup White Wine
- Sea Salt & Black Pepper to Taste
- 6 Cherrystone Clams, Cleaned
- 4 Ounces Tilapia, Sliced into 1 Inch Strips
- 4 Ounces Dry Sea Scallops
- 1/8 Cup Parmesan Cheese, Grated
- 1/2 Teaspoon Marjoram, Chopped & Fresh

Directions:

1. Get a pot of water and bring it to a boil, cooking your pasta until tender which should take roughly eight minutes. Drain and then rinse your pasta.
2. Heat your oil using a large skillet over medium heat, and then once your oil is hot add in your garlic and shallot. Cook for a minute, and stir often.
3. Increase the heat to medium-high before adding your salt, wine, pepper and tomatoes, bringing it to a simmer. Cook for one minute more.
4. Add your clams next, covering and cooking for another two minutes.
5. Stir in your marjoram, scallops and fish next. Cover, and cook until the fish is done all the way through and your clams have opened up.t his will take up to five minutes, and get rid of any clams that do not open.
6. Spoon the sauce and your clams over the pasta, sprinkling with parmesan and marjoram before serving. Serve warm.

GINGER SHRIMP & TOMATO RELISH

Serves: 2

Time: 25 Minutes

Ingredients:

- 1 1/2 Tablespoons Vegetable Oil
- 1 Clove Garlic, Minced
- 10 Shrimp, Extra Large, Peeled & Tails Left On
- 3/4 Tablespoons Finger, Grated & Peeled
- 1 Green Tomatoes, Halved
- 2 Plum Tomatoes, Halved
- 1 Tablespoon Lime Juice, Fresh
- 1/2 Teaspoon Sugar
- 1/2 Tablespoon Jalapeno with Seeds, Fresh & Minced
- 1/2 Tablespoon Basil, Fresh & Chopped
- 1/2 Tablespoons Cilantro, Chopped & Fresh
- 10 Skewers
- Sea Salt & Black Pepper to Taste

Directions:

1. Soak your skewers in a pan of water for at least a half hour.
2. Stir your garlic and ginger together in a bowl, transferring half to a larger bowl and stirring it with two tablespoons of your oil. Add in the shrimp, and make sure they are well coated.
3. Cover and place it in the fridge for at least a half hour, and then allow it to refrigerate.

4. Heat your grill to high, and grease the grates lightly using oil. Get out a bowl and toss your plum and green tomatoes with the remaining tablespoon of oil, seasoning with salt and pepper.

5. Grill your tomatoes with the cut side up and the skins should be charred. The flesh of your tomato should be tender, which will take about four to six minutes for the plum tomato and about ten minutes for the green tomato.

6. Remove the skins once the tomatoes are cool enough to handle, and then discard the seeds. Chop the tomatoes flesh fine, adding it to the reserved ginger and garlic. Add in your sugar, jalapeno, lime juice and basil.

7. Season your shrimp using salt and pepper threading them onto the skewers, and then grill until they turn opaque, which is about two minutes on each side. Place the shrimp on a platter with your relish and enjoy.

Serves: 2

Time: 20 Minutes

Ingredients:

- 2 Cups Angel Hair Pasta, Cooked
- 1/2 lb. Medium Shrimp, Peeled
- 1 Clove Garlic, Minced
- 1 Cup Tomato, Chopped
- 1 Teaspoon Olive Oil
- 1/6 Cup Kalamata Olives, Pitted & Chopped
- 1/8 Cup Basil, Fresh & Sliced Thin
- 1 Tablespoon Capers, Drained
- 1/8 Cup Feta Cheese, Crumbled
- Dash Black Pepper

Directions:

1. Cook your pasta per package instructions, and then heat up your olive oil in a skillet using medium-high heat. Cook your garlic for half a minute, and then add your shrimp. Sauté for a minute more.
2. Add your basil and tomato, and then reduce the heat to allow it to simmer for three minutes. Your tomato should be tender.
3. Stir in your olives and capers. Add a dash of black pepper, and combine your shrimp mix and pasta together to serve. Top with cheese before serving warm.

POACHED COD

Serves: 2

Time: 35 Minutes

Ingredients:

- 2 Cod Filets, 6 Ounces
- Sea Salt & Black Pepper to Taste
- 1/4 Cup Dry White Wine
- 1/4 Cup Seafood Stock
- 2 Cloves Garlic, Minced
- 1 Bay Leaf
- 1/2 Teaspoon Sage, Fresh & Chopped
- 2 Rosemary Sprigs to Garnish

Directions:

1. Start by turning your oven to 375, and then season the fillets with salt and pepper. Place them in a baking pan, and add in your stock, garlic, wine, sage and bay leaf. Cover well, and then bake for twenty minutes. Your fish should be flaky when tested with a fork.
2. Use a spatula to remove each fillet, placing the liquid over high heat and cooking to reduce in half. This should take ten minutes, and you need to stir frequently.
3. Serve dripped in poaching liquid and garnished with a rosemary sprig.

Serves: 2

Time: 15 Minutes

Ingredients:

- 2 lbs. Live Mussels, Fresh
- 1 Cup Dry White Wine
- 1/4 Teaspoon Sea Salt, Fine
- 3 Cloves Garlic, Minced
- 2 Teaspoons Shallots, Diced
- 1/4 Cup Parsley, Fresh & Chopped, Divided
- 2 Tablespoons olive Oil
- 1/4 Lemon, Juiced

Directions:

1. Get out a colander and scrub your mussels, rinsing them using cold water. Discard mussels that will not close if they're tapped, and then use a paring knife to remove the beard from each one.

2. Get out stockpot, placing it over medium-high heat, and add in your garlic, shallots, wine and parsley. Bring it to a simmer. Once it's at a steady simmer, add in your mussels and cover. Allow them to simmer for five to seven minutes. Make sure they do not overcook.

3. Use a slotted spoon to remove them, and add your lemon juice and olive oil into the pot. Stir well, and pour the broth over your mussels before serving with parsley.

DILLY SALMON

Serves: 2

Time: 25 Minutes

Ingredients:

- 2 Salmon Fillets, 6 Ounces Each
- 1 Tablespoon Olive Oil
- 1/2 Tangerine, Juiced
- 2 Teaspoons Orange Zest
- 2 Tablespoons Dill, Fresh & Chopped
- Sea Salt & Black Pepper to Taste

Directions:

1. Start by heating your oven to 375, and then get out two ten-inch pieces of foil. Rub your filets down with olive oil on both side before seasoning with salt and pepper, placing each fillet into a piece of foil.

2. Drizzle your orange juice over each one, and then top with orange zest and dill. Fold your packet closed, making sure it has two inches of air space within the foil so your fish can steam, and then place them on a baking dish.

3. Bake for fifteen minutes before opening the packets, and transfer to two serving plates. Pour the sauce over the top of each before serving.

CHICKEN & VEGETABLE SOUP

Serves: 2

Time: 30 Minutes

Ingredients:

- 1/2 Cup Parsley, Fresh & Chopped + More for Garnish
- 1 Teaspoon Olive Oil
- 1 Yellow Onion, Diced
- 1 Carrot, Large, Peeled & Diced
- 1 Celery Stalk, Peeled & diced
- 2 Chicken Breasts, Boneless, Skinless, 6 Ounces Each & Cut into 1-inch Pieces
- 1 Zucchini, Diced
- 2 Yellow Squash, Diced
- 1 Teaspoon Basil, Fresh & Chopped
- 2 Cups Chicken Stock
- Sea Salt & Black Pepper to Taste

Directions:

1. Get out a heavy skillet and heat your olive oil over medium-high heat. Add in your celery, onion and carrot. Sauté for five minutes, making sure to sit frequently. Add in your chicken, cooking for another ten minutes while stirring often.

2. Add in your squash and zucchini before mixing in your basil, parsley and oregano. Season with salt and pepper, and cook for five minutes. Reduce the heat, and pour in the stock. Cover, cooking for another ten minutes.

3. Ladle into bowl and serve garnished with parsley.

SIDE DISHES & SNACKS

SAUTÉED SPINACH & PINE NUTS

Serves: 2

Time: 10 Minutes

Ingredients:

- 10 Ounce Bag Spinach, Fresh
- 2 Tablespoons Golden Raisins
- 2 Cloves Garlic, Minced
- 2 Teaspoons Olive Oil
- 1 Tablespoon Parmesan Cheese, Shaved
- 1 Tablespoon Pine Nuts
- 2 Teaspoons Balsamic Vinegar
- Sea Salt & Black Pepper to Taste

Directions:

1. Heat the oil in a skillet using medium-high heat, and then cook your garlic, raisin and pine nuts for a half a minute. Stir well to keep from burning, and then add in your spinach. Cover your pan and allow it to wilt for two minutes.
2. Remove from heat, and then add in your vinegar and salt.
3. Top with cheese and pepper before serving.

FRENCH ONION SOUP

Serves: 2

Time: 30 Minutes

Ingredients:

- 8 Ounces Chickpeas, Rinsed
- 14 Ounces Beef Broth, Reduced Sodium
- 1 Tablespoon Olive Oil
- 1 Small Sweet Onion, Sliced
- 1 Tablespoon Sherry
- 1 Leek, Chopped
- 1/2 Teaspoon Thyme, Fresh & Chopped
- 2 Tablespoons Garlic, Chopped
- 2 Slices Whole Wheat Bread, Toasted
- 2 Tablespoons Chives, Fresh & Minced
- 1/3 Cup Gruyere, Shredded
- Black Pepper to Taste

Directions:

1. Heat your oil in a skillet using medium-high heat. Add in your onion, and then reduce to medium to cook stir often until it's softened and brown. This will take up to eight minutes.

2. Throw in your garlic, thyme and leek, cooking for four minutes more. Stir often.

3. Add in the pepper and sherry, and then increase it to medium-high heat again. Stir well and cook until almost all of the liquid has evaporated. This will take less than a minute, and then stir in your broth and chickpeas. Bring it to a boil, and reduce the heat to allow it to simmer. Cook until the vegetables are tender, which will take three minutes. Remove from heat before stirring in the chives.

4. Place your bread at the bottom of two bowls, topping with cheese and ladling your soup over each one.

BRAISED KALE & TOMATOES

Serves: 2

Time: 20 Minutes

Ingredients:

- 1/2 lb. Kale, Chopped
- 2 Cloves Garlic, Sliced Thin
- 1 Teaspoon Olive Oil
- 1/2 Cup Cherry Tomatoes, Halved
- 1/4 Cup Vegetable Stock
- 1/2 Tablespoon Lemon Juice, Fresh
- Sea Salt & Black Pepper to Taste

Directions:

1. Heat your olive oil in a frying pan using medium heat, and then sauté your garlic for two minutes.
2. Add in your vegetable stock and kale, and then cover. Reduce the heat to medium-low, and allow it to wilt. It will take five minutes.
3. Stir in your tomatoes, and cook uncovered for seven minutes. Remove from heat, and season with salt, pepper and lemon juice before serving warm.

ANCHOVY & OLIVE SALAD

Serves: 2

Time: 40 Minutes

Ingredients:

- 3 Anchovy Fillets
- 1/2 Small Red Onion, Sliced Thin
- 8 Black Olives, Salt Cured, Pitted & Halved
- 2 Small Blood Oranges
- 1 1/2 Tablespoons Olive Oil
- 1/2 Tablespoon Lemon Juice, Fresh
- 1 Teaspoon Fennel Fronts, Minced Fine
- 1/2 Tablespoon Lemon Juice, Fresh
- 1/8 Teaspoon Black Pepper

Directions:

1. Peel the orange carefully and cut away the membrane and pith. Make sure to capture all the juices, and slice the oranges into rounds.
2. Arrange them on a platter, and reserve the juice in a bowl. Distribute your onions over the oranges, and then top with olive and anchovy fillets. Drizzle with oil, and let it marinate for a half hour before serving sprinkled with fennel fronts.

Serves: 2

Time: 2 Hours 30 Minutes

Ingredients:

- 1 Cube Chicken Bouillon
- 3 Pantoates, Peeled & Quartered
- 1/6 Cup Olive Oil
- 1 Clove Garlic, Chopped Fine
- 3/4 Cup Water
- 1/8 Cup Lemon Juice, Fresh
- 1/2 Teaspoon Thyme
- 1/2 Teaspoon Rosemary
- Sea Salt & Black Pepper to Taste

Directions:

1. Start by heating your oven to 350.
2. Mix your olive oil, thyme, garlic, rosemary, pepper, lemon juice, bouillon and water in a bowl.
3. Arrange the potatoes in a baking dish, pouring the mixture over them, and bake for one and a half to two hours. Turn occasionally to keep from burning, and serve warm.

Serves: 2

Time: 50 Minutes

Ingredients:

- 1 Shallot, Sliced
- 1 Small Eggplant
- 1 1/2 Tablespoons Sherry Wine Vinegar
- 1 Clove Garlic, Minced
- 1/2 Tablespoon Sugar
- 1 Tablespoon Golden Raisins
- Dash Red Pepper Flakes
- 1/2 Tablespoon Capers
- 1/8 Cup + 2 Teaspoons Olive Oil
- 2 Gaeta Olives, Pitted & Chopped
- Vegetable Oil
- Sea Salt to Taste

Directions:

1. Slice the eggplant crosswise, slicing it into eight slices. Sprinkle with salt, and then place the pieces in a colander. Allow them to drain for a half hour, and then rinse the eggplant off before patting it dry.

2. Get out a sauce pan and place it over medium heat. Add your red pepper flakes, vinegar, sugar, garlic, shallots, sugar and two tablespoons of water. Bring it to a boil, cooking for a minute before taking it off of heat. Stir in your capers, olives, raisins, and 1/8 cup olive oil. Mix well and allow it to cool to room temperature.

3. Heat the grill to high, and make sure to oil the grates using vegetable oil. Brush the eggplant with two teaspoons of olive oil. Cook the eggplant until charred and tender. Turn it halfway through.

4. Arrange it on a platter, spooning the shallot mixture on top to serve.

MEDITERRANEAN FRIED RICE

Serves: 2

Time: 15 Minutes

Ingredients:

- 3/4 Cup Rice, Cooked
- 1 Clove Garlic, Minced
- 1 Tablespoon Olive Oil
- 5 Ounces Chopped Spinach, Thawed & Drained
- 1/4 Cup Feta Cheese with Herbs, Crumbled
- 2 Ounces Roasted Red Pepper, Drained & Chopped
- 3 Ounce Marinated Artichoke Hearts, Drained & Quartered

Directions:

1. Start by heating your olive oil over medium heat in a skillet and then add in your garlic. Cook for two minutes, and then add in your rice. Cook for an additional two minutes and make sure to stir frequently to keep it from burning.
2. Add in the spinach, cooking for an additional three minutes, and then stir in your roasted red peppers. Add the artichoke hearts, cooking for an additional two minutes.
3. Throw in the feta and mix before removing from heat. Serve warm.

Serves: 2

Time: 15 Minutes

Ingredients:

- 3/4 lb. Swiss Chard
- 1/2 Yellow Onion, Sliced
- 1/2 Jalapeno Pepper, Chopped Fine
- 1/6 Cup Kalamata Olives, Pitted & Chopped
- 1/2 Teaspoon Olive Oil
- 1/4 Cup Water

Directions:

1. Remove he stem of your Swiss chard from your leaves, and chop the leaves. Set them to the side and cut the stem into one-inch pieces.
2. Get out a skillet and place your oil over medium heat, adding in your onion, garlic and jalapeno. Cook until your onion becomes translucent. This will take roughly six minutes.
3. Add in your olives, water and swiss chard. Cover the skillet, cooking for three minutes more. Stir until the swiss chard leaves and steam are tender, which takes about five more minutes.

CUCUMBER & PESTO BOATS

Serves: 2

Time: 20 Minutes

Ingredients:

- 2 Small Cucumbers
- 1/4 Teaspoon Sea Salt, Fine
- 1/2 Cup Basil, Fresh & Packed
- 1 Clove Garlic, Minced
- 1/8 Cup Walnut Pieces
- 1/8 Cup Parmesan Cheese, Grated
- 1/8 Cup Olive Oil
- 1/4 Teaspoon Paprika

Directions:

1. Cut your cucumbers in half lengthwise, and again crosswise to make four pieces each. Use a spoon to hollow the seeds out and create a shell. Salt each piece, putting it to the side.
2. Get out a blender and combine your garlic, basil, walnuts, olive oil and parmesan. Blend until it makes a smooth mixture, and then spread it over your "boats". Sprinkle with paprika before serving.

CITRUS MELON

Serves: 2

Time: 4 Hours 10 Minutes

Ingredients:

- 1 Cups Melon, Cubed (Sharlyn, Crenshaw or Honeydew)
- 1 Cup Cantaloupe, Cubed
- 1/4 Cup Orange Juice, Fresh
- 1/8 Cup Lime Juice, Fresh
- 1/2 Tablespoon Orange Zest

Directions:

1. Combine both melons in a bowl, and then get out a small bow whisk your orange zest, lime juice and orange juice together. Pour it over your fruit, and mix well.
2. Cover and allow it to set in the fridge for four hours. You'll need to stir occasionally. Serve cold.

DESSERT RECIPES

YOGURT MOUSSE & SOUR CHERRY TOPPING

Serves: 2

Time: 4 Hours 20 Minutes

Ingredients:

- 1/2 Cup Heavy Cream, Well Chilled
- 3 Ounces Yogurt, Plain & Unsweetened
- 1/4 Teaspoon Vanilla Extract, Pure
- 1 Tablespoon Gelatin, Unflavored
- 3 Tablespoons Sugar
- 1 Cup Sour Cherry, Pureed Slightly

Directions:

1. Get out a small saucepan, and then sprinkle in your gelatin over ¼ cup of cold water, allowing it to soften for a minute. Heat your mixture using low heat, and stir until all of the gelatin powder has dissolved.
2. Blend your sugar, vanilla and sour cherry puree into the gelatin mix, making sure it's mixed well.
3. Transfer it to a bowl, and then stir the yogurt in.
4. Beat the cream until stiff peaks form. Fold in the cherry mixture, and then let it set in the fridge for four hours. Garnish with drained cherry preserves before serving chilled.

CARAMEL ROASTED FIGS

Serves: 2

Time: 45 Minutes

Ingredients:

- 1/4 Cup Sugar
- Whipped Cream
- 6 Figs, Ripe but Slightly Firm

Directions:

1. Start by heating the oven to 450, and then get out a baking dish. Rinse your figs and then arrange them on the baking dish standing up.

2. Get out a skillet and then pour in your sugar, making sure it's spread evenly over the bottom. Put it over medium-low heat.

3. The sugar should start to melt around the edges, and then shake the pan, and continue to let it melt. The sugar will turn a deep honey color, and then start tilting, swirling and shaking to distribute the sugar evenly. Don't poke at it, and make sure to be patient.

4. All of your sugar should be completely melted and turning an amber color. This will take about fifteen minutes.

5. Pour this over your figs, and then roast until big bubbles form and the caramel turns a deep amber. This should take about fifteen minutes more. Serve garnished with whipped cream.

Serves: 2

Time: 1 Hour 10 Minutes

Ingredients:

- 1/4 Cup Pomegranate Seeds
- 3/4 Cup Pomegranate Juice
- 1/2 Cup Sweet Dessert Wine
- 2 Bosc Pears, Ripe & Firm

Directions:

1. Pele your pears, and then leave them whole. The steam should be intact, and then slice off the bases so that they stand upright, and then use a cover to remove the cores, working form the base up.

2. Put your pears on the sides in a saucepan, and pour in your pomegranate juice and wine. Bring it to a simmer using medium-high heat, and then cover. Reduce the heat to low, simmering until the pears turn tender. This will take thirty to forty-five minutes, and you should turn them once or even twice to make sure that they color evenly.

3. Remove them from the skillet using a slotted spoon, and then place them in a shallow bowl.

4. Boil the liquid over high heat until it thickens and is reduced to roughly a half a cup, which will take up to twenty minutes.

5. Spoon a tablespoon of this sauce over each pear, and then sprinkle with pomegranate seeds before serving.

MARINATED BERRIES

Serves: 2

Time: 20 Minutes

Ingredients:

- 2 Shortbread Biscuits
- 1/2 Cup Blueberries, Fresh
- 1/2 Cup Raspberries, Fresh
- 1/2 Cup Strawberries, Sliced
- 1 Teaspoon Vanilla Extract, Pure
- 2 Tablespoons Brown Sugar
- 1/4 Cup Balsamic Vinegar

Directions:

1. Get out a bowl and whisk your vanilla, brown sugar and balsamic vinegar together.
2. In a different bowl add your raspberries, blueberries and strawberries together, pouring the vinegar mixture over it.
3. Allow it to marinate for fifteen minutes, and then serve over shortbread.

Serves: 2

Time: 10 Minutes

Ingredients:

- 1 Tablespoon Almonds, Toasted & Chopped
- 6 Figs, Fresh
- 1 1/2 Teaspoons Honey, Raw
- 3 Tablespoons Mascarpone Cheese
- 1/2 Teaspoon Vanilla Extract, Pure
- 1/4 Teaspoon Orange Zest
- 1/2 Teaspoon Mint, Fresh & Chopped

Directions:

1. Take a half inch off of each of your figs from the top. Cut a thin slice off the bottom so they can stand up. Cut an x into the tops of the fig, making sure they're ¾ inch deep. Open the figs from the top but don't break them all the way open.
2. Combine the vanilla, honey and mascarpone into a bowl. Spoon the mixture into your figs, and drizzle with a half a teaspoon of honey. Top with mint, almonds and orange zest before serving.

ROASTED HONEY APPLES

Serves: 2

Time: 45 Minutes

Ingredients:

- 1 Teaspoon Olive Oil
- 1/2 Teaspoon Sea Salt, Fine
- 4 Apples, Firm, Peeled, Cored & Sliced
- 1 1/2 Teaspoons Cinnamon, Divided
- 2 Tablespoon Milk, Low Fat
- 2 Tablespoons Honey, Raw

Directions:

1. Start by heating your oven to 375, and then get out a small casserole dish. Grease it using olive oil, and then get out a bowl.

2. In your bowl toss the apple slices with salt and a half a teaspoon of cinnamon, placing them in the baking dish. Bake for twenty minutes.

3. While your apples are baking get out a saucepan and heat your honey, milk and remaining cinnamon using medium heat. Stir frequently, and allow it to simmer. Remove it from the pan, and then serve warm.

BAKED PEARS IN RED WINE

Serves: 2

Time: 1 Hour 35 Minutes

Ingredients:

- 2 Pears, Firm
- 1/2 Cup Sweet Red Wine
- 1 Small Cinnamon Stick
- 1 Teaspoon Light Brown Sugar
- 1/4 Teaspoon Almond Extract, Pure
- 2 Mint Sprigs for Garnish

Directions:

1. Start by heating your oven to 325, and then peel your pears. Leave the core and stem there. Cut a slice from the bottom of each so that they stand up well. Place them in a small baking dish.
2. Get out a small saucepan and combine your cinnamon stick, red wine and brown sugar. Heat it using low heat and allow it to simmer. Once simmering, stir in almond extract and remove your cinnamon stick. Pour the liquid into the baking dish, and slide the dish into the oven. Make sur that the pears do not tip over.
3. Bake until they are fork tender and golden, which should take roughly one hour. The bottom half of the pears should turn a deep red.
4. Transfer to a platter and pour the red wine into the saucepan, heating over medium heat. Allow it to reduce by half, which will take an additional fifteen minutes.
5. Remove the pan from over heat, and then allow it to cool for the minutes before serving drizzled in the red wine sauce and garnished with mint.

SUMMER GRANITA

Serves: 2

Time: 1 Hour 40 Minutes

Ingredients:

- 1/2 Cup Raspberries, Fresh
- 1/2 Cup Blackberries, Fresh
- 1/2 Teaspoon Lemon Juice, Fresh
- 1/2 Cup Strawberries, Fresh
- 1/8 Cup Sugar

Directions:

1. Get out a small saucepan, and then pour a cup of water in. Bring it to a boil using high heat, adding in sugar. Mix and allow it to dissolve.

2. Remove the pan from heat, and then add in your lemon juice and berries, allowing it to come to room temperature. Once it's been cooled blend on high using an immersion blender until smooth.

3. Pour the puree into a baking dish, and then allow it to freeze for an hour.

4. Stir with a fork every thirty minutes.

5. Serve like you would ice cream.

SEAFOOD & FISH RECIPES

MEDITERRANEAN FISH FILLETS

Preparation Time: 10 minutes

Cooking Time: 3 minutes

Servings: 4

INGREDIENTS

- 4 cod fillets
- 1 lb grape tomatoes, halved
- 1 cup olives, pitted and sliced
- 2 tbsp capers
- 1 tsp dried thyme
- 2 tbsp olive oil
- 1 tsp garlic, minced
- Pepper
- Salt

DIRECTIONS

1. Pour 1 cup water into the instant pot then place steamer rack in the pot.
2. Spray heat-safe baking dish with cooking spray.
3. Add half grape tomatoes into the dish and season with pepper and salt.
4. Arrange fish fillets on top of cherry tomatoes. Drizzle with oil and season with garlic, thyme, capers, pepper, and salt.
5. Spread olives and remaining grape tomatoes on top of fish fillets.
6. Place dish on top of steamer rack in the pot.
7. Seal pot with a lid and select manual and cook on high for 3 minutes.
8. Once done, release pressure using quick release. Remove lid.
9. Serve and enjoy.

NUTRITION: Calories 212 Fat 11.9 g Carbohydrates 7.1 g Sugar 3 g Protein 21.4 g Cholesterol 55 mg

FLAVORS CIOPPINO

Preparation Time: 10 minutes

Cooking Time: 5 minutes

Servings: 6

INGREDIENTS

- 1 lb codfish, cut into chunks
- 1 1/2 lbs shrimp
- 28 oz can tomatoes, diced
- 1 cup dry white wine
- 1 bay leaf
- 1 tsp cayenne
- 1 tsp oregano
- 1 shallot, chopped
- 1 tsp garlic, minced
- 1 tbsp olive oil
- 1/2 tsp salt

DIRECTIONS

1. Add oil into the inner pot of instant pot and set the pot on sauté mode.
2. Add shallot and garlic and sauté for 2 minutes.
3. Add wine, bay leaf, cayenne, oregano, and salt and cook for 3 minutes.
4. Add remaining ingredients and stir well.
5. Seal pot with a lid and select manual and cook on low for 0 minutes.
6. Once done, release pressure using quick release. Remove lid.
7. Serve and enjoy.

NUTRITION: Calories 281 Fat 5 g Carbohydrates 10.5 g Sugar 4.9 g Protein 40.7 g Cholesterol 266 mg

DELICIOUS SHRIMP ALFREDO

Preparation Time: 10 minutes

Cooking Time: 3 minutes

Servings: 4

INGREDIENTS

- 12 shrimp, remove shells
- 1 tbsp garlic, minced
- 1/4 cup parmesan cheese
- 2 cups whole wheat rotini noodles
- 1 cup fish broth
- 15 oz alfredo sauce
- 1 onion, chopped
- Salt

DIRECTIONS

1. Add all ingredients except parmesan cheese into the instant pot and stir well.
2. Seal pot with lid and cook on high for 3 minutes.
3. Once done, release pressure using quick release. Remove lid.
4. Stir in cheese and serve.

NUTRITION: Calories 669 Fat 23.1 g Carbohydrates 76 g Sugar 2.4 g Protein 37.8 g Cholesterol 190 mg

TOMATO OLIVE FISH FILLETS

Preparation Time: 10 minutes

Cooking Time: 8 minutes

Servings: 4

INGREDIENTS

- 2 lbs halibut fish fillets
- 2 oregano sprigs
- 2 rosemary sprigs
- 2 tbsp fresh lime juice
- 1 cup olives, pitted
- 28 oz can tomatoes, diced
- 1 tbsp garlic, minced
- 1 onion, chopped
- 2 tbsp olive oil

DIRECTIONS

1. Add oil into the inner pot of instant pot and set the pot on sauté mode.
2. Add onion and sauté for 3 minutes.
3. Add garlic and sauté for a minute.
4. Add lime juice, olives, herb sprigs, and tomatoes and stir well.
5. Seal pot with lid and cook on high for 3 minutes.
6. Once done, release pressure using quick release. Remove lid.
7. Add fish fillets and seal pot again with lid and cook on high for 2 minutes.
8. Once done, release pressure using quick release. Remove lid.
9. Serve and enjoy.

NUTRITION: Calories 333 Fat 19.1 g Carbohydrates 31.8 g Sugar 8.4 g Protein 13.4 g Cholesterol 5 mg

SHRIMP SCAMPI

Preparation Time: 10 minutes

Cooking Time: 8 minutes

Servings: 6

INGREDIENTS

- 1 lb whole wheat penne pasta
- 1 lb frozen shrimp
- 2 tbsp garlic, minced
- 1/4 tsp cayenne
- 1/2 tbsp Italian seasoning
- 1/4 cup olive oil
- 3 1/2 cups fish stock
- Pepper
- Salt

DIRECTIONS

1. Add all ingredients into the inner pot of instant pot and stir well.
2. Seal pot with lid and cook on high for 6 minutes.
3. Once done, release pressure using quick release. Remove lid.
4. Stir well and serve.

NUTRITION: Calories 435 Fat 12.6 g Carbohydrates 54.9 g Sugar 0.1 g Protein 30.6 g Cholesterol 116 mg

EASY SALMON STEW

Preparation Time: 10 minutes

Cooking Time: 8 minutes

Servings: 6

INGREDIENTS

- 2 lbs salmon fillet, cubed
- 1 onion, chopped
- 2 cups fish broth
- 1 tbsp olive oil
- Pepper
- salt

DIRECTIONS

1. Add oil into the inner pot of instant pot and set the pot on sauté mode.
2. Add onion and sauté for 2 minutes.
3. Add remaining ingredients and stir well.
4. Seal pot with lid and cook on high for 6 minutes.
5. Once done, release pressure using quick release. Remove lid.
6. Stir and serve.

NUTRITION: Calories 243 Fat 12.6 g Carbohydrates 0.8 g Sugar 0.3 g Protein 31 g Cholesterol 78 mg

ITALIAN TUNA PASTA

Preparation Time: 10 minutes

Cooking Time: 5 minutes

Servings: 6

INGREDIENTS

- 15 oz whole wheat pasta
- 2 tbsp capers
- 3 oz tuna
- 2 cups can tomatoes, crushed
- 2 anchovies
- 1 tsp garlic, minced
- 1 tbsp olive oil
- Salt

DIRECTIONS

1. Add oil into the inner pot of instant pot and set the pot on sauté mode.
2. Add anchovies and garlic and sauté for 1 minute.
3. Add remaining ingredients and stir well. Pour enough water into the pot to cover the pasta.
4. Seal pot with a lid and select manual and cook on low for 4 minutes.
5. Once done, release pressure using quick release. Remove lid.
6. Stir and serve.

NUTRITION: Calories 339 Fat 6 g Carbohydrates 56.5 g Sugar 5.2 g Protein 15.2 g Cholesterol 10 mg

GARLICKY CLAMS

Preparation Time: 10 minutes

Cooking Time: 5 minutes

Servings: 4

INGREDIENTS

- 3 lbs clams, clean
- 4 garlic cloves
- 1/4 cup olive oil
- 1/2 cup fresh lemon juice
- 1 cup white wine
- Pepper
- Salt

DIRECTIONS

1. Add oil into the inner pot of instant pot and set the pot on sauté mode.
2. Add garlic and sauté for 1 minute.
3. Add wine and cook for 2 minutes.
4. Add remaining ingredients and stir well.
5. Seal pot with lid and cook on high for 2 minutes.
6. Once done, allow to release pressure naturally. Remove lid.
7. Serve and enjoy.

NUTRITION: Calories 332 Fat 13.5 g Carbohydrates 40.5 g Sugar 12.4 g Protein 2.5 g Cholesterol 0 mg

DELICIOUS FISH TACOS

Preparation Time: 10 minutes

Cooking Time: 8 minutes

Servings: 8

INGREDIENTS

- 4 tilapia fillets
- 1/4 cup fresh cilantro, chopped
- 1/4 cup fresh lime juice
- 2 tbsp paprika
- 1 tbsp olive oil
- Pepper
- Salt

DIRECTIONS

1. Pour 2 cups of water into the instant pot then place steamer rack in the pot.
2. Place fish fillets on parchment paper.
3. Season fish fillets with paprika, pepper, and salt and drizzle with oil and lime juice.
4. Fold parchment paper around the fish fillets and place them on a steamer rack in the pot.
5. Seal pot with lid and cook on high for 8 minutes.
6. Once done, release pressure using quick release. Remove lid.
7. Remove fish packet from pot and open it.
8. Shred the fish with a fork and serve.

NUTRITION: Calories 67 Fat 2.5 g Carbohydrates 1.1 g Sugar 0.2 g Protein 10.8 g Cholesterol 28 mg

PESTO FISH FILLET

Preparation Time: 10 minutes

Cooking Time: 8 minutes

Servings: 4

INGREDIENTS

- 4 halibut fillets
- 1/2 cup water
- 1 tbsp lemon zest, grated
- 1 tbsp capers
- 1/2 cup basil, chopped
- 1 tbsp garlic, chopped
- 1 avocado, peeled and chopped
- Pepper
- Salt

DIRECTIONS

1. Add lemon zest, capers, basil, garlic, avocado, pepper, and salt into the blender blend until smooth.
2. Place fish fillets on aluminum foil and spread a blended mixture on fish fillets.
3. Fold foil around the fish fillets.
4. Pour water into the instant pot and place trivet in the pot.
5. Place foil fish packet on the trivet.
6. Seal pot with lid and cook on high for 8 minutes.
7. Once done, allow to release pressure naturally. Remove lid.
8. Serve and enjoy.

NUTRITION: Calories 426 Fat 16.6 g Carbohydrates 5.5 g Sugar 0.4 g Protein 61.8 g Cholesterol 93 mg

TUNA RISOTTO

Preparation Time: 10 minutes

Cooking Time: 23 minutes

Servings: 6

INGREDIENTS

- 1 cup of rice
- 1/3 cup parmesan cheese, grated
- 1 1/2 cups fish broth
- 1 lemon juice
- 1 tbsp garlic, minced
- 1 onion, chopped
- 2 tbsp olive oil
- 2 cups can tuna, cut into chunks
- Pepper
- Salt

DIRECTIONS

1. Add oil into the inner pot of instant pot and set the pot on sauté mode.
2. Add garlic, onion, and tuna and cook for 3 minutes.
3. Add remaining ingredients except for parmesan cheese and stir well.
4. Seal pot with lid and cook on high for 20 minutes.
5. Once done, release pressure using quick release. Remove lid.
6. Stir in parmesan cheese and serve.

NUTRITION: Calories 228 Fat 7 g Carbohydrates 27.7 g Sugar 1.2 g Protein 12.6 g Cholesterol 21 mg

SALSA FISH FILLETS

Preparation Time: 10 minutes

Cooking Time: 2 minutes

Servings: 4

INGREDIENTS

- 1 lb tilapia fillets
- 1/2 cup salsa
- 1 cup of water
- Pepper
- Salt

DIRECTIONS

1. Place fish fillets on aluminum foil and top with salsa and season with pepper and salt.
2. Fold foil around the fish fillets.
3. Pour water into the instant pot and place trivet in the pot.
4. Place foil fish packet on the trivet.
5. Seal pot with lid and cook on high for 2 minutes.
6. Once done, release pressure using quick release. Remove lid.
7. Serve and enjoy.

NUTRITION: Calories 342 Fat 10.5 g Carbohydrates 41.5 g Sugar 1.9 g Protein 18.9 g Cholesterol 31 mg

COCONUT CLAM CHOWDER

Preparation Time: 10 minutes

Cooking Time: 7 minutes

Servings: 6

INGREDIENTS

- 6 oz clams, chopped
- 1 cup heavy cream
- 1/4 onion, sliced
- 1 cup celery, chopped
- 1 lb cauliflower, chopped
- 1 cup fish broth
- 1 bay leaf
- 2 cups of coconut milk
- Salt

DIRECTIONS

1. Add all ingredients except clams and heavy cream and stir well.
2. Seal pot with lid and cook on high for 5 minutes.
3. Once done, release pressure using quick release. Remove lid.
4. Add heavy cream and clams and stir well and cook on sauté mode for 2 minutes.
5. Stir well and serve.

NUTRITION: Calories 301 Fat 27.2 g Carbohydrates 13.6 g Sugar 6 g Protein 4.9 g Cholesterol 33 mg

FETA TOMATO SEA BASS

Preparation Time: 10 minutes

Cooking Time: 8 minutes

Servings: 4

INGREDIENTS

- 4 sea bass fillets
- 1 1/2 cups water
- 1 tbsp olive oil
- 1 tsp garlic, minced
- 1 tsp basil, chopped
- 1 tsp parsley, chopped
- 1/2 cup feta cheese, crumbled
- 1 cup can tomatoes, diced
- Pepper
- Salt

DIRECTIONS

1. Season fish fillets with pepper and salt.
2. Pour 2 cups of water into the instant pot then place steamer rack in the pot.
3. Place fish fillets on steamer rack in the pot.
4. Seal pot with lid and cook on high for 5 minutes.
5. Once done, release pressure using quick release. Remove lid.
6. Remove fish fillets from the pot and clean the pot.
7. Add oil into the inner pot of instant pot and set the pot on sauté mode.
8. Add garlic and sauté for 1 minute.
9. Add tomatoes, parsley, and basil and stir well and cook for 1 minute.
10. Add fish fillets and top with crumbled cheese and cook for a minute.
11. Serve and enjoy.

NUTRITION: Calories 219 Fat 10.1 g Carbohydrates 4 g Sugar 2.8 g Protein 27.1 g Cholesterol 70 mg

STEWED MUSSELS & SCALLOPS

Preparation Time: 10 minutes

Cooking Time: 11 minutes

Servings: 4

INGREDIENTS

- 2 cups mussels
- 1 cup scallops
- 2 cups fish stock
- 2 bell peppers, diced
- 2 cups cauliflower rice
- 1 onion, chopped
- 1 tbsp olive oil
- Pepper
- Salt

DIRECTIONS

1. Add oil into the inner pot of instant pot and set the pot on sauté mode.
2. Add onion and peppers and sauté for 3 minutes.
3. Add scallops and cook for 2 minutes.
4. Add remaining ingredients and stir well.
5. Seal pot with lid and cook on high for 6 minutes.
6. Once done, allow to release pressure naturally. Remove lid.
7. Stir and serve.

NUTRITION: Calories 191 Fat 7.4 g Carbohydrates 13.7 g Sugar 6.2 g Protein 18 g

Cholesterol 29 mg

HEALTHY HALIBUT SOUP

Preparation Time: 10 minutes

Cooking Time: 13 minutes

Servings: 4

INGREDIENTS

- 1 lb halibut, skinless, boneless, & cut into chunks
- 2 tbsp ginger, minced
- 2 celery stalks, chopped
- 1 carrot, sliced
- 1 onion, chopped
- 1 cup of water
- 2 cups fish stock
- 1 tbsp olive oil
- Pepper
- Salt

DIRECTIONS

1. Add oil into the inner pot of instant pot and set the pot on sauté mode.
2. Add onion and sauté for 3-4 minutes.
3. Add water, celery, carrot, ginger, and stock and stir well.
4. Seal pot with lid and cook on high for 5 minutes.
5. Once done, release pressure using quick release. Remove lid.
6. Add fish and stir well. Seal pot again and cook on high for 4 minutes.
7. Once done, release pressure using quick release. Remove lid.
8. Stir and serve.

NUTRITION: Calories 4586 Fat 99.6 g Carbohydrates 6.3 g Sugar 2.1 g Protein 861 g Cholesterol 1319 mg

CREAMY FISH STEW

Preparation Time: 10 minutes

Cooking Time: 8 minutes

Servings: 6

INGREDIENTS

- 1 lb white fish fillets, cut into chunks
- 2 tbsp olive oil
- 1 cup kale, chopped
- 1 cup cauliflower, chopped
- 1 cup broccoli, chopped
- 3 cups fish broth
- 1 cup heavy cream
- 2 celery stalks, diced
- 1 carrot, sliced
- 1 onion, diced
- Pepper
- Salt

DIRECTIONS

1. Add oil into the inner pot of instant pot and set the pot on sauté mode.
2. Add onion and sauté for 3 minutes.
3. Add remaining ingredients except for heavy cream and stir well.
4. Seal pot with lid and cook on high for 5 minutes.
5. Once done, allow to release pressure naturally. Remove lid.
6. Stir in heavy cream and serve.

NUTRITION: Calories 296 Fat 19.3 g Carbohydrates 7.5 g Sugar 2.6 g Protein 22.8 g Cholesterol 103 mg

NUTRITIOUS BROCCOLI SALMON

Preparation Time: 10 minutes

Cooking Time: 4 minutes

Servings: 4

INGREDIENTS

- 4 salmon fillets
- 10 oz broccoli florets
- 1 1/2 cups water
- 1 tbsp olive oil
- Pepper
- Salt

DIRECTIONS

1. Pour water into the instant pot then place steamer basket in the pot.
2. Place salmon in the steamer basket and season with pepper and salt and drizzle with oil.
3. Add broccoli on top of salmon in the steamer basket.
4. Seal pot with lid and cook on high for 4 minutes.
5. Once done, release pressure using quick release. Remove lid.
6. Serve and enjoy.

NUTRITION: Calories 290 Fat 14.7 g Carbohydrates 4.7 g Sugar 1.2 g Protein 36.5 g Cholesterol 78 mg

SHRIMP ZOODLES

Preparation Time: 10 minutes

Cooking Time: 5 minutes

Servings: 4

INGREDIENTS

- 2 zucchini, spiralized
- 1 lb shrimp, peeled and deveined
- 1/2 tsp paprika
- 1 tbsp basil, chopped
- 1/2 lemon juice
- 1 tsp garlic, minced
- 2 tbsp olive oil
- 1 cup vegetable stock
- Pepper
- Salt

DIRECTIONS

1. Add oil into the inner pot of instant pot and set the pot on sauté mode.
2. Add garlic and sauté for a minute.
3. Add shrimp and lemon juice and stir well and cook for 1 minute.
4. Add remaining ingredients and stir well.
5. Seal pot with lid and cook on high for 3 minutes.
6. Once done, release pressure using quick release. Remove lid.
7. Serve and enjoy.

NUTRITION: Calories 215 Fat 9.2 g Carbohydrates 5.8 g Sugar 2 g Protein 27.3 g Cholesterol 239 mg

HEALTHY CARROT & SHRIMP

Preparation Time: 10 minutes

Cooking Time: 6 minutes

Servings: 4

INGREDIENTS

- 1 lb shrimp, peeled and deveined
- 1 tbsp chives, chopped
- 1 onion, chopped
- 1 tbsp olive oil
- 1 cup fish stock
- 1 cup carrots, sliced
- Pepper
- Salt

DIRECTIONS

1. Add oil into the inner pot of instant pot and set the pot on sauté mode.
2. Add onion and sauté for 2 minutes.
3. Add shrimp and stir well.
4. Add remaining ingredients and stir well.
5. Seal pot with lid and cook on high for 4 minutes.
6. Once done, release pressure using quick release. Remove lid.
7. Serve and enjoy.

NUTRITION: Calories 197 Fat 5.9 g Carbohydrates 7 g Sugar 2.5 g Protein 27.7 g Cholesterol 239 mg

SALMON WITH POTATOES

Preparation Time: 10 minutes

Cooking Time: 15 minutes

Servings: 4

INGREDIENTS

- 1 1/2 lbs Salmon fillets, boneless and cubed
- 2 tbsp olive oil
- 1 cup fish stock
- 2 tbsp parsley, chopped
- 1 tsp garlic, minced
- 1 lb baby potatoes, halved
- Pepper
- Salt

DIRECTIONS

1. Add oil into the inner pot of instant pot and set the pot on sauté mode.
2. Add garlic and sauté for 2 minutes.
3. Add remaining ingredients and stir well.
4. Seal pot with lid and cook on high for 13 minutes.
5. Once done, release pressure using quick release. Remove lid.
6. Serve and enjoy.

NUTRITION: Calories 362 Fat 18.1 g Carbohydrates 14.5 g Sugar 0 g Protein 37.3 g Cholesterol 76 mg

HONEY GARLIC SHRIMP

Preparation Time: 10 minutes

Cooking Time: 5 minutes

Servings: 4

INGREDIENTS

- 1 lb shrimp, peeled and deveined
- 1/4 cup honey
- 1 tbsp garlic, minced
- 1 tbsp ginger, minced
- 1 tbsp olive oil
- 1/4 cup fish stock
- Pepper
- Salt

DIRECTIONS

1. Add shrimp into the large bowl. Add remaining ingredients over shrimp and toss well.

2. Transfer shrimp into the instant pot and stir well.

3. Seal pot with lid and cook on high for 5 minutes.

4. Once done, release pressure using quick release. Remove lid.

5. Serve and enjoy.

NUTRITION: Calories 240 Fat 5.6 g Carbohydrates 20.9 g Sugar 17.5 g Protein 26.5 g Cholesterol 239 mg

SIMPLE LEMON CLAMS

Preparation Time: 10 minutes

Cooking Time: 10 minutes

Servings: 4

INGREDIENTS

- 1 lb clams, clean
- 1 tbsp fresh lemon juice
- 1 lemon zest, grated
- 1 onion, chopped
- 1/2 cup fish stock
- Pepper
- Salt

DIRECTIONS

1. Add all ingredients into the inner pot of instant pot and stir well.
2. Seal pot with lid and cook on high for 10 minutes.
3. Once done, release pressure using quick release. Remove lid.
4. Serve and enjoy.

NUTRITION: Calories 76 Fat 0.6 g Carbohydrates 16.4 g Sugar 5.4 g Protein 1.8 g Cholesterol 0 mg

CRAB STEW

Preparation Time: 10 minutes

Cooking Time: 13 minutes

Servings: 2

INGREDIENTS

- 1/2 lb lump crab meat
- 2 tbsp heavy cream
- 1 tbsp olive oil
- 2 cups fish stock
- 1/2 lb shrimp, shelled and chopped
- 1 celery stalk, chopped
- 1/2 tsp garlic, chopped
- 1/4 onion, chopped
- Pepper
- Salt

DIRECTIONS

1. Add oil into the inner pot of instant pot and set the pot on sauté mode.
2. Add onion and sauté for 3 minutes.
3. Add garlic and sauté for 30 seconds.
4. Add remaining ingredients except for heavy cream and stir well.
5. Seal pot with lid and cook on high for 10 minutes.
6. Once done, release pressure using quick release. Remove lid.
7. Stir in heavy cream and serve.

NUTRITION: Calories 376 Fat 25.5 g Carbohydrates 5.8 g Sugar 0.7 g Protein 48.1 g Cholesterol 326 mg

HONEY BALSAMIC SALMON

Preparation Time: 10 minutes

Cooking Time: 3 minutes

Servings: 2

INGREDIENTS

- 2 salmon fillets
- 1/4 tsp red pepper flakes
- 2 tbsp honey
- 2 tbsp balsamic vinegar
- 1 cup of water
- Pepper
- Salt

DIRECTIONS

1. Pour water into the instant pot and place trivet in the pot.
2. In a small bowl, mix together honey, red pepper flakes, and vinegar.
3. Brush fish fillets with honey mixture and place on top of the trivet.
4. Seal pot with lid and cook on high for 3 minutes.
5. Once done, release pressure using quick release. Remove lid.
6. Serve and enjoy.

NUTRITION: Calories 303 Fat 11 g Carbohydrates 17.6 g Sugar 17.3 g Protein 34.6 g Cholesterol 78 mg

SPICY TOMATO CRAB MIX

Preparation Time: 10 minutes

Cooking Time: 12 minutes

Servings: 4

INGREDIENTS

- 1 lb crab meat
- 1 tsp paprika
- 1 cup grape tomatoes, cut into half
- 2 tbsp green onion, chopped
- 1 tbsp olive oil
- Pepper
- Salt

DIRECTIONS

7. Add oil into the inner pot of instant pot and set the pot on sauté mode.
8. Add paprika and onion and sauté for 2 minutes.
9. Add the rest of the ingredients and stir well.
10. Seal pot with lid and cook on high for 10 minutes.
11. Once done, release pressure using quick release. Remove lid.
12. Serve and enjoy.

NUTRITION: Calories 142 Fat 5.7 g Carbohydrates 4.3 g Sugar 1.3 g Protein 14.7 g Cholesterol 61 mg

DIJON FISH FILLETS

Preparation Time: 10 minutes

Cooking Time: 3 minutes

Servings: 2

INGREDIENTS

- 2 white fish fillets
- 1 tbsp Dijon mustard
- 1 cup of water
- Pepper
- Salt

DIRECTIONS

1. Pour water into the instant pot and place trivet in the pot.
2. Brush fish fillets with mustard and season with pepper and salt and place on top of the trivet.
3. Seal pot with lid and cook on high for 3 minutes.
4. Once done, release pressure using quick release. Remove lid.
5. Serve and enjoy.

NUTRITION: Calories 270 Fat 11.9 g Carbohydrates 0.5 g Sugar 0.1 g Protein 38 g Cholesterol 119 mg

LEMONEY PRAWNS

Preparation Time: 10 minutes

Cooking Time: 3 minutes

Servings: 2

INGREDIENTS

- 1/2 lb prawns
- 1/2 cup fish stock
- 1 tbsp fresh lemon juice
- 1 tbsp lemon zest, grated
- 1 tbsp olive oil
- 1 tbsp garlic, minced
- Pepper
- Salt

DIRECTIONS

1. Add all ingredients into the inner pot of instant pot and stir well.
2. Seal pot with lid and cook on high for 3 minutes.
3. Once done, release pressure using quick release. Remove lid.
4. Drain prawns and serve.

NUTRITION: Calories 215 Fat 9.5 g Carbohydrates 3.9 g Sugar 0.4 g Protein 27.6 g Cholesterol 239 mg

LEMON COD PEAS

Preparation Time: 10 minutes

Cooking Time: 10 minutes

Servings: 4

INGREDIENTS

- 1 lb cod fillets, skinless, boneless and cut into chunks
- 1 cup fish stock
- 1 tbsp fresh parsley, chopped
- 1/2 tbsp lemon juice
- 1 green chili, chopped
- 3/4 cup fresh peas
- 2 tbsp onion, chopped
- Pepper
- Salt

DIRECTIONS

1. Add all ingredients into the inner pot of instant pot and stir well.
2. Seal pot with lid and cook on high for 10 minutes.
3. Once done, release pressure using quick release. Remove lid.
4. Stir and serve.

NUTRITION: Calories 128 Fat 1.6 g Carbohydrates 5 g Sugar 2.1 g Protein 23.2 g Cholesterol 41 mg

QUICK & EASY SHRIMP

Preparation Time: 10 minutes

Cooking Time: 1 minute

Servings: 6

DIRECTIONS

- 1 3/4 lbs shrimp, frozen and deveined
- 1/2 cup fish stock
- 1/2 cup apple cider vinegar
- Pepper
- Salt

DIRECTIONS

1. Add all ingredients into the inner pot of instant pot and stir well.
2. Seal pot with lid and cook on high for 1 minute.
3. Once done, release pressure using quick release. Remove lid.
4. Stir and serve.

NUTRITION: Calories 165 Fat 2.4 g Carbohydrates 2.2 g Sugar 0.1 g Protein 30.6 g Cholesterol 279 mg

CREAMY CURRY SALMON

Preparation time: 10 minutes

Cooking time: 20 minutes

Servings: 2

INGREDIENTS

- 2 salmon fillets, boneless and cubed
- 1 tablespoon olive oil
- 1 tablespoon basil, chopped
- Sea salt and black pepper to the taste
- 1 cup Greek yogurt
- 2 teaspoons curry powder
- 1 garlic clove, minced
- ½ teaspoon mint, chopped

DIRECTIONS

1. Heat up a pan with the oil over medium-high heat, add the salmon and cook for 3 minutes.
2. Add the rest of the ingredients, toss, cook for 15 minutes more, divide between plates and serve.

NUTRITION: Calories 284, fat 14.1, fiber 8.5, carbs 26.7, protein 31.4

MAHI MAHI AND POMEGRANATE SAUCE

Preparation time: 10 minutes

Cooking time: 10 minutes

Servings: 4

INGREDIENTS

- 1 and ½ cups chicken stock
- 1 tablespoon olive oil
- 4 mahi mahi fillets, boneless
- 4 tablespoons tahini paste
- Juice of 1 lime
- Seeds from 1 pomegranate
- 1 tablespoon parsley, chopped

DIRECTIONS

1. Heat up a pan with the oil over medium-high heat, add the fish and cook for 3 minutes on each side.
2. Add the rest of the ingredients, flip the fish again, cook for 4 minutes more, divide everything between plates and serve.

NUTRITION: Calories 224, fat 11.1, fiber 5.5, carbs 16.7, protein 11.4

SMOKED SALMON AND VEGGIES MIX

Preparation time: 10 minutes

Cooking time: 20 minutes

Servings: 4

INGREDIENTS

- 3 red onions, cut into wedges
- ¾ cup green olives, pitted and halved
- 3 red bell peppers, roughly chopped
- ½ teaspoon smoked paprika
- Salt and black pepper to the taste
- 3 tablespoons olive oil
- 4 salmon fillets, skinless and boneless
- 2 tablespoons chives, chopped

DIRECTIONS

1. In a roasting pan, combine the salmon with the onions and the rest of the ingredients, introduce in the oven and bake at 390 degrees F for 20 minutes.
2. Divide the mix between plates and serve.

NUTRITION: Calories 301, fat 5.9, fiber 11.9, carbs 26.4, protein 22.4

SALMON AND MANGO MIX

Preparation time: 10 minutes

Cooking time: 25 minutes

Servings: 2

INGREDIENTS

- 2 salmon fillets, skinless and boneless
- Salt and pepper to the taste
- 2 tablespoons olive oil
- 2 garlic cloves, minced
- 2 mangos, peeled and cubed
- 1 red chili, chopped
- 1 small piece ginger, grated
- Juice of 1 lime
- 1 tablespoon cilantro, chopped

DIRECTIONS

1. In a roasting pan, combine the salmon with the oil, garlic and the rest of the ingredients except the cilantro, toss, introduce in the oven at 350 degrees F and bake for 25 minutes.

2. Divide everything between plates and serve with the cilantro sprinkled on top.

NUTRITION: Calories 251, fat 15.9, fiber 5.9, carbs 26.4, protein 12.4

SALMON AND CREAMY ENDIVES

Preparation time: 10 minutes

Cooking time: 15 minutes

Servings: 4

INGREDIENTS

- 4 salmon fillets, boneless
- 2 endives, shredded
- Juice of 1 lime
- Salt and black pepper to the taste
- ¼ cup chicken stock
- 1 cup Greek yogurt
- ¼ cup green olives pitted and chopped
- ¼ cup fresh chives, chopped
- 3 tablespoons olive oil

DIRECTIONS

1. Heat up a pan with half of the oil over medium heat, add the endives and the rest of the ingredients except the chives and the salmon, toss, cook for 6 minutes and divide between plates.

2. Heat up another pan with the rest of the oil, add the salmon, season with salt and pepper, cook for 4 minutes on each side, add next to the creamy endives mix, sprinkle the chives on top and serve.

NUTRITION: Calories 266, fat 13.9, fiber 11.1, carbs 23.8, protein 17.5

TROUT AND TZATZIKI SAUCE

Preparation time: 10 minutes

Cooking time: 10 minutes

Servings: 4

INGREDIENTS

- Juice of ½ lime
- Salt and black pepper to the taste
- 1 and ½ teaspoon coriander, ground
- 1 teaspoon garlic, minced
- 4 trout fillets, boneless
- 1 teaspoon sweet paprika
- 2 tablespoons avocado oil

- For the sauce:
- 1 cucumber, chopped
- 4 garlic cloves, minced
- 1 tablespoon olive oil
- 1 teaspoon white vinegar
- 1 and ½ cups Greek yogurt
- A pinch of salt and white pepper

DIRECTIONS

1. Heat up a pan with the avocado oil over medium-high heat, add the fish, salt, pepper, lime juice, 1 teaspoon garlic and the paprika, rub the fish gently and cook for 4 minutes on each side.

2. In a bowl, combine the cucumber with 4 garlic cloves and the rest of the ingredients for the sauce and whisk well.

3. Divide the fish between plates, drizzle the sauce all over and serve with a side salad.

NUTRITION: Calories 393, fat 18.5, fiber 6.5, carbs 18.3, protein 39.6

PARSLEY TROUT AND CAPERS

Preparation time: 10 minutes

Cooking time: 10 minutes

Servings: 4

INGREDIENTS

- 4 trout fillets, boneless
- 3 ounces tomato sauce
- A handful parsley, chopped
- 2 tablespoons olive oil
- Salt and black pepper to the taste

DIRECTIONS

1. Heat up a pan with the oil over medium-high heat, add the fish, salt and pepper and cook for 3 minutes on each side.

2. Add the rest of the ingredients, cook everything for 4 minutes more.

3. Divide everything between plates and serve.

NUTRITION: Calories 308, fat 17, fiber 1, carbs 3, protein 16

BAKED TROUT AND FENNEL

Preparation time: 10 minutes

Cooking time: 22 minutes

Servings: 4

INGREDIENTS

- 1 fennel bulb, sliced
- 2 tablespoons olive oil
- 1 yellow onion, sliced
- 3 teaspoons Italian seasoning
- 4 rainbow trout fillets, boneless
- ¼ cup panko breadcrumbs
- ½ cup kalamata olives, pitted and halved
- Juice of 1 lemon

DIRECTIONS

1. Spread the fennel the onion and the rest of the ingredients except the trout and the breadcrumbs on a baking sheet lined with parchment paper, toss them and cook at 400 degrees F for 10 minutes.

2. Add the fish dredged in breadcrumbs and seasoned with salt and pepper and cook it at 400 degrees F for 6 minutes on each side.

3. Divide the mix between plates and serve.

NUTRITION: Calories 306, fat 8.9, fiber 11.1, carbs 23.8, protein 14.5

LEMON RAINBOW TROUT

Preparation time: 10 minutes

Cooking time: 15 minutes

Servings: 2

INGREDIENTS

- 2 rainbow trout
- Juice of 1 lemon
- 3 tablespoons olive oil
- 4 garlic cloves, minced
- A pinch of salt and black pepper

DIRECTIONS

1. Line a baking sheet with parchment paper, add the fish and the rest of the ingredients and rub.

2. Bake at 400 degrees F for 15 minutes, divide between plates and serve with a side salad.

NUTRITION: Calories 521, fat 29, fiber 5, carbs 14, protein 52

TROUT AND PEPPERS MIX

Preparation time: 10 minutes

Cooking time: 20 minutes

Servings: 4

INGREDIENTS

- 4 trout fillets, boneless
- 2 tablespoons kalamata olives, pitted and chopped
- 1 tablespoon capers, drained
- 2 tablespoons olive oil
- A pinch of salt and black pepper
- 1 and ½ teaspoons chili powder
- 1 yellow bell pepper, chopped
- 1 red bell pepper, chopped
- 1 green bell pepper, chopped

DIRECTIONS

1. Heat up a pan with the oil over medium-high heat, add the trout, salt and pepper and cook for 10 minutes.

2. Flip the fish, add the peppers and the rest of the ingredients, cook for 10 minutes more, divide the whole mix between plates and serve.

NUTRITION: Calories 572, fat 17.4, fiber 6, carbs 71, protein 33.7

COD AND CABBAGE

Preparation time: 10 minutes

Cooking time: 15 minutes

Servings: 4

INGREDIENTS

- 3 cups green cabbage, shredded
- 1 sweet onion, sliced
- A pinch of salt and black pepper
- ½ cup feta cheese, crumbled
- 4 teaspoons olive oil
- 4 cod fillets, boneless
- ¼ cup green olives, pitted and chopped

DIRECTIONS

1. Grease a roasting pan with the oil, add the fish, the cabbage and the rest of the ingredients, introduce in the pan and cook at 450 degrees F for 15 minutes.

2. Divide the mix between plates and serve.

NUTRITION: Calories 270, fat 10, fiber 3, carbs 12, protein 31

MEDITERRANEAN MUSSELS

Preparation time: 10 minutes

Cooking time: 10 minutes

Servings: 4

INGREDIENTS

- 1 white onion, sliced
- 3 tablespoons olive oil
- 2 teaspoons fennel seeds
- 4 garlic cloves, minced
- 1 teaspoon red pepper, crushed
- A pinch of salt and black pepper
- 1 cup chicken stock
- 1 tablespoon lemon juice
- 2 and ½ pounds mussels, scrubbed
- ½ cup parsley, chopped
- ½ cup tomatoes, cubed

DIRECTIONS

1. Heat up a pan with the oil over medium-high heat, add the onion and the garlic and sauté for 2 minutes.

2. Add the rest of the ingredients except the mussels, stir and cook for 3 minutes more.

3. Add the mussels, cook everything for 6 minutes more, divide everything into bowls and serve.

NUTRITION: Calories 276, fat 9.8, fiber 4.8, carbs 6.5, protein 20.5

MUSSELS BOWLS

Preparation time: 10 minutes

Cooking time: 10 minutes

Servings: 4

INGREDIENTS

- 2 pounds mussels, scrubbed
- 1 tablespoon garlic, minced
- 1 tablespoon basil, chopped
- 1 yellow onion, chopped
- 6 tomatoes, cubed
- 1 cup heavy cream
- 2 tablespoons olive oil
- 1 tablespoon parsley, chopped

DIRECTIONS

1. Heat up a pan with the oil over medium-high heat, add the garlic and the onion and sauté for 2 minutes.
2. Add the mussels and the rest of the ingredients, toss, cook for 7 minutes more, divide into bowls and serve.

NUTRITION: Calories 266, fat 11.8, fiber 5.8, carbs 16.5, protein 10.5

CALAMARI AND DILL SAUCE

Preparation time: 10 minutes

Cooking time: 15 minutes

Servings: 4

INGREDIENTS

- 1 and ½ pound calamari, sliced into rings
- 10 garlic cloves, minced
- 2 tablespoons olive oil
- Juice of 1 and ½ lime
- 2 tablespoons balsamic vinegar
- 3 tablespoons dill, chopped
- A pinch of salt and black pepper

DIRECTIONS

1. Heat up a pan with the oil over medium-high heat, add the garlic, lime juice and the other ingredients except the calamari and cook for 5 minutes.
2. Add the calamari rings, cook everything for 10 minutes more, divide between plates and serve.

NUTRITION: Calories 282, fat 18.6, fiber 4, carbs 9.2, protein 18.5

CHILI CALAMARI AND VEGGIE MIX

Preparation time: 10 minutes

Cooking time: 40 minutes

Servings: 4

INGREDIENTS

- 1 pound calamari rings
- 2 red chili peppers, chopped
- 2 tablespoons olive oil
- 3 garlic cloves, minced
- 14 ounces canned tomatoes, chopped
- 2 tablespoons tomato paste
- 1 tablespoon thyme, chopped
- Salt and black pepper to the taste
- 2 tablespoons capers, drained
- 12 black olives, pitted and halved

DIRECTIONS

1. Heat up a pan with the oil over medium-high heat, add the garlic and the chili peppers and sauté for 2 minutes.
2. Add the rest of the ingredients except the olives and capers, stir, bring to a simmer and cook for 22 minutes.
3. Add the olives and capers, cook everything for 15 minutes more, divide everything into bowls and serve.

NUTRITION: Calories 274, fat 11.6, fiber 2.8, carbs 13.5, protein 15.4

CPSIA information can be obtained
at www.ICGtesting.com
Printed in the USA
BVHW091029210721
612411BV00014B/4235